"Tom Nisbett has captured the spirit of the mountain trail and the spirit of life in *Retreat Upward*. Like gold embedded in rock, there are precious nuggets of life-truths that will challenge you to search within for those character qualities that are only discovered and developed through resistance and gravity—two forces most present on the mountain trail and on the trail of life. Tom challenged and encouraged me to retreat upward and outward, and I encourage you to do the same! I know you will enjoy the climb!"

–LEE S. FERGUSON,

retired CFO and VP for financial affairs, East Texas Baptist University

"*Retreat Upward* is an intimate peek into an experienced climber's heart and mind—one might even say his soul. Tom Nisbett calls us to 'retreat upward,' but he comes alongside to help us discover more of ourselves and, in doing so, to enlarge our soul."

–TIM DINGER,

executive clinical director, John Brown University

"Tom Nisbett through personal conquest leads us on a journey of the soul. In his poetic-style journal, Tom explores facing the hardship of the elements while continuing to press on to the summit as an act of faith. The personal encounters explored, especially that of father and son illuminates our spiritual desire to know and grow in relationship with the father."

–KEN SUTTERFIELD,

Christian camping/ministry leader

"I'm grateful for this collection of stories from Tom Nisbett's climbing adventures and the perspective and soul wisdom he has found on the mountain top. This book is like a spiritual retreat of equal parts memoir and contemplative meditations on what it means to journey further up and further in and to ascend to joy. It makes me want to climb a mountain to find this kind of wisdom for myself."

—MATTHEW CLEVELAND,
chief development officer, Arkansas Sheriffs' Youth Ranches

"*Retreat Upward* is a spiritual testimony about mountaineering. This book will bring you to tears, make you smile with great gratitude, and make you strive every day to wake up in every way and know the love going out and the love coming in God divinely provided for us in natural landscapes."

—MELANIE ANNE BADEN,
author of *Skullgrass: A Safe Haven*

Retreat Upward

Retreat Upward

A Mountain Pathway for the Soul

THOMAS NISBETT

RESOURCE *Publications* • Eugene, Oregon

RETREAT UPWARD
A Mountain Pathway for the Soul

Resource Publications
An Imprint of Wipf and Stock Publishers
199 W. 8th Ave., Suite 3
Eugene, OR 97401

www.wipfandstock.com

PAPERBACK ISBN: 979-8-3852-1951-3
HARDCOVER ISBN: 979-8-3852-1952-0
EBOOK ISBN: 979-8-3852-1953-7

06/06/24

To my climbing companions in life

In ancient times, YHWH—the name of Israel's deity—said to Abram, "Go from your country . . . to the land I will show you." People who act on faith "go." And there is personal courage in "going."

Contents

Mountains and Natural Elements List

1. Elbert   Fire
2. Humphries   Wind
3. Whitney   Terrain
4. Granite   Earth
5. Shasta   Snow
6. Montserrat   Sky
7. Comapedrosa Water
8. Wheeler   Spirit
9. Harvard   Night

Abstract

"Retreat Upward" is a Wallace Stegner expression meaning "Go to the mountains" and implies strenuous physical effort on foot ascending and descending on trails and beyond trails. Retreats are primarily about getting away from physical work for reflection or renewal by focusing on the work of the soul, the inner person. A spiritual retreat involves taking a rest, stepping off life's treadmill. How does the physical act of hiking and climbing up a mountain trail to reach challenging vistas combine rigor and renewal while engaging the soul?

The mountain pathway can be a metaphor for living since it lifts our vision and provides a higher perspective above the valleys of life, not without struggle and effort. There exists the mountain you see and the mountain you don't see, the outer life and the inner life. It's a path worth traveling to explore the outer limits of this inner world, and better understand your own pathway. The author combines insights from nine mountains and nine elements of nature, with short stories from a dozen more personal climbs.

Preface

My mother was born under a tree on the eastern slope of the Sandia Mountains in May 1918 just six years after New Mexico became a state. My father was born in that same year near Stephenville, Texas, and moved to New Mexico for some of his childhood years. They convinced me that I was born in a small-town hospital but got outdoors as quickly as I could. I loved our backyard treehouse.

The friends in my neighborhood dug tunnels and trenches and built fortresses in the West Texas sandy loam. We camped at Rita Blanca Lake when we were old enough to ride our bikes a mile or so into the local canyons. Summer vacations were always spent in Northern New Mexico or Southern Colorado where my love of mountains was born. I loved tent-camping beside a mountain stream.

In winter the heavy snowfalls that dropped out of the Rockies into the Texas Panhandle provided snow cave building opportunities to sleep outside. Climbing to the top of our outside television antenna, I could see the snowstorms coming. Life patterns form early. *Some patterns we choose, and some patterns choose us.*

Hiking and climbing mountains in the Sangre de Cristo Range started before the age of ten for me as did retreats called "Family Camp" every August at Ceta Canyon Church Camp. A spiritual retreat can provide a mountaintop experience as can a solo climb on a great mountain. There exists no guarantee. We may love mountaintop experiences, but we know that faith must be lived out in all the daily rhythms of life. We all have a mountain or two in our lives, challenges we face.

The mountain and climbing it can be a metaphor for living since it lifts our vision and provides a higher perspective, above the valleys of life, not without struggle and effort. There is the mountain you see and the mountain you don't see, false summits and actual summits, the outer life and the inner life. *Adventure is not outside mankind, it is within. (Eliot)*

"Retreat" sounds like taking a rest, stepping off the treadmill of life. Spiritual retreats are often about getting away from work for reflection and renewal by attending to the work of the soul, the inner person. "Retreat Upward" implies strenuous work. How does the physical act of walking or hiking up a mountain trail really engage and enlarge the soul?

My friend Bruce in Tennessee posted this wisdom: "The moments that made yesterday are now replaced by this moment in the here and now. The next moments will come and go as well. How they affect me is *within reach if only I will reach within*." Every mountain climb has taught me that in life I must reach within, not only to draw on inner strength, but to keep reaching for the essential.

Whatever pathway in nature helps you reach within—garden, desert, mountain, ocean—one can find portals between the outer life and the inner life. Nature can teach you if you listen. Parker Palmer writes, " . . . for millennia the world's wisdom traditions have majored in mapping various pathways to the soul. A close friend of mine says, "we do not have a soul, we are a soul." This book, though not a map, is for souls.

The world does not always fall into divisible realms but is often an unmappable mesh of interrelations. (Macfarlane) Are there wilderness jurisdictions to be aware of on the mountain pathway? Sure. Is map-reading an important backcountry skill? Yes. But as Yvon Chouinard once quipped on his Bhutan Expedition, *Burn the map.* Learn to read the visible elements of mountains and identify the invisible forces with which we contend, inevitably bound together.

I discovered an invisible mountain bond with my mother who was born in mid-May and never did hike nor climb:

The Land of Enchantment[*]
Born in New Mexico
Beneath a timeless tree, where the sunflowers
Grow bright yellow and gold
And the mountains give way to the valleys below . . .

The sun danced across the meadow
So close to your mother, so close to the earth
You know a Greater Spirit was there
Witnessing your birth . . .

Your mountain streams flow through my blood
They carry your dreams, autumn changing leaves,
And flood my memories with love . . .

This collection of mountain stories reflects a spirit of exploring, though rightly labeled a memoir. My dad shows up throughout the book because he was my friend and mentor, a great example of a good, good father. You need a few trusted climbing companions in the mountains of life. And while the mountains form a theme in my writing, they symbolize something much more solid, more eternal.

[*] Nisbett, *Mountains, Hills, and Prairies.*

Mt. Elbert, Colorado

Photo taken by Hogs555 as seen from Turquoise Lake.
https://commons.wikimedia.org/wiki/File:Mt._Elbert.jpg

ONE

Going Out

Going out is really going in.
The longest journey is the journey inward.

Climbing in Colorado in September is a spectacular season for hiking a wilderness trail, beneath bluebird skies among golden aspen trees. If your timing is bad and you encounter a late-summer thunderstorm or an early blizzard, then, you add the right layer! Most years a big high-pressure system lingers there making the weather dry and tranquil. My Colorado climbing trips are usually in the Autumn and yet, my first ascent of Mount Elbert occurred in July 1999. We took a midsummer hike on the mountain pathway.

In May of that year my dad celebrated his 81st birthday. He had come late to the 50 Peaks Challenge—reaching the state highpoint in all 50 states—when he had discovered the idea only seven years earlier. He and I were great friends and so we started hiking the easy highpoints whenever we got a chance.

Most of the ones we did together were in or near our Great Plains region and Dad knew he could do the hikes—Black Mesa in

Oklahoma, Guadalupe Peak in Texas, Mt. Magazine in Arkansas, Driskill Mountain in Louisiana, as well as two mountains from several years earlier, Wheeler Peak in New Mexico and Clingman's Dome in Tennessee.

By June 1999, we were considering a climb of Mount Elbert, the highest mountain in Colorado at 14,433 feet. It would be Dad's attempt on his highest mountain so far. We needed to do it together and we needed a good plan. We also needed Mom's consent.

Dad would be fine I told her—he had completed the New York City Marathon at age 68, hiked 14–15 state highpoints, and run many 5K, 10K, and half-marathon races in this later season of his life. We wrote out an itinerary and then Dad and I drove from his home in Dalhart, Texas, to Buena Vista, Colorado, on July 5th.

We had made this trip many times over the years from camping trips in Northern New Mexico to summer hiking in Southern Colorado. One year my wife Lou Ann joined us for a climb in the Weminuche Wilderness in Colorado when the monsoon rains soaked all our gear and clothing. After 3–4 days of rainy skies, Lou Ann wasn't feeling well and needed some sunshine. We all happily packed up and drove home. A simple pregnancy test revealed that she was "with child," our daughter Mallary.

Dad and I loved traveling together and having great conversations. I am a talker, and he was a good listener. We enjoyed each other's company so much that even a long stretch without conversation was life-giving. We were comfortable with silence, a gift from the wilderness.

Our seven-hour drive to central Colorado went by quickly and we arrived in Buena Vista by early afternoon since we had always headed west for the mountains before daybreak. We were both early-risers, and all my childhood mountain trips began in the dark. I grew up with no fear of the pre-dawn darkness.

We had reserved a small log cabin in Buena Vista where we checked in and got settled. Knowing Dad like I did we agreed to rest awhile, and then made some coffee. Dad took his coffee black and enjoyed many cups until midday. *Let's drink some coffee and get after it. (Galen Rowell)*

Dad lived at 4000 feet elevation for over 40 years, so he always did well at altitude. He began running there in his mid-fifties and was in great shape. Our first day's plan in Colorado was to walk and jog two miles at 8000 feet. Check. We both felt good.

On July 6th, we loaded the truck and drove up to Halfmoon Creek campground in the San Isabel National Forest at 10,240 feet to set up camp near the Mt. Elbert Trailhead. We met a group of teenage boys from an outdoor program who had already climbed Elbert that morning—3.5 hours up and 2 hours down.

Their group had a flat tire on their passenger van in the uneven parking lot, so they were looking for a square rock or block of wood to place under the tire jack. I loaned them my big thick study bible that I had with me, and it worked perfectly. One of them commented, "Well, finally the Bible is good for something."

As soon as we got our camp ready, an afternoon rain shower began in the typical Colorado summer pattern. We felt good so we put on our raingear and followed our Day 2 plan to acclimate by hiking to tree line or above. Dad was hiking well as we approached 12,000 feet and our turn-around point.

We talked about helping the young hikers change their flat tire and how so many bibles sit on a table or bookshelf unused. Dad added, "God's word lifts our souls and today it lifted a vehicle." *I will lift my eyes up to the hills . . . My help comes from God.* For Dad . . . going out was going in.

On July 7th, I got up about 4:30 am to clear night skies and a bluebird weather forecast. The rain was gone! I heated water on my small MSR stove for coffee and oatmeal and woke up Dad. After a light breakfast and gear check, we left the Elbert TH at 5:30 that morning. Dad was hiking well at age 81 and we slowly ascended the trail to the tree line. The Class 1 trail continues above the lodgepole pine forests to the crest of Elbert's northeast ridge.

Special mountain climbing experience is not necessary on the well-worn trail to the top. Most summers the sun has melted all the snow there, but we did encounter a few large patches of snow as we neared the summit. Dad was a little unsteady, so he used some trekking poles to help him cross the snow sections.

We reached Elbert's summit at noon after 6.5 hours of hiking up the mountain gaining 4500 vertical feet over the 4.5 miles. The weather was perfect, and the skies were clear blue all morning with some clouds building up by noon. We took some pictures and recorded our names in the logbook. Nine or ten people were on top when we were there, and we saw probably 25–30 hikers all day. We stayed on the summit for thirty minutes and then began our slow descent through the rocky, snowy section which covered the upper trail.

It took us a little over four hours to return to camp and Dad's toenails were getting as black as his coffee. It was a long and strenuous hike of 11 hours for a guy in his 80s. Dad was a gentle and patient man. He had to summon the will and the tenacity to keep going but he never doubted that he could do it. Dad had the desire or "fire in his belly" to complete this highpoint and at age 81 he was still finding the outer limits of his inner world. *The longest journey is the journey inward.*

The not so visible aspects attributed to fire are understood as energy, desire, or *fire in the belly* and represent intangible or immeasurable forces within us. I love the picture of a small child face-to-face with a fierce lion and the caption reading: *Crisis doesn't produce character. It reveals character.* Character is built on the inside of a person and often is built invisibly. There is no place like the steep mountain pathway for revealing inner strength.

When my son Shawn was ten years old, Dad and I planned a climb with him to New Mexico's highest point—Wheeler Peak at 13,161 feet. Did the ten-year old get tired of the climb? Did he wonder out loud if this mountain had a summit? Did he want to quit at times? Sure! We encouraged him and monitored his physical signs and he had to dig deep to meet the mental challenge. Climbing is character-forming, providing a pathway to the soul and inner resources. Crises will come in life, and they will reveal if character is present within. Relaxing on a beach doesn't do that.

The *visible* aspects of fire—heat, light, smoke, and a deterrent to wild animals—are familiar to wilderness campers and backpackers and those who watch survivor shows. Most people love a warm fire. At our home we have a large outdoor stone fireplace, a small chiminea on the front deck, and an indoor fireplace. I regularly gather and chop wood for a fire. The warmth from a campfire and its light will push back the darkness.

A forest fire burning out of control and leaving destruction in its path is an image visible more and more as people have populated and built houses in pristine natural settings. In the nation's forests and wilderness, the benefits of controlled burns usually lower the risk of larger uncontrolled fires while killing pests to keep trees healthy. The burned underbrush and vegetation supplies nitrogen and nutrients to the forest floor. *Fire is a visible and natural element and often a warning.*

Climbing in the San Juan Mountain Range of southwestern Colorado in September 2018, we could smell the smoke of recent fires as we rode the Durango & Silverton train from Durango to our drop-off for the Needleton Whistlestop and our trailhead to the Chicago Basin.

The coal-burning narrow-gauge train was most likely the culprit months earlier as its sparks ignited dry grass along the route up to Silverton. They had to stop running for a few months in the height of tourist season. It goes without saying, we built no campfires in the backcountry on that trip.

A few years earlier, backpacking in the Wind River Range of Wyoming, we built a huge campfire to celebrate our climb of Wyoming's highest mountain, Gannett Peak. I have had many memorable campfires, council fires, and bonfires but this one sticks in my memory. It kept the wild animals at a distance and warmed our bodies after the glacial climbing. We burned a huge supply of dry wood and talked late into the night. That was a *visible* fire.

The visible and invisible aspects of the fire element combine to give light and energy to your soul. Going into the wilderness of mountains and the wild backcountry is a pathway for my soul-energy, an inward journey as well as outward adventure.

May your trails be crooked, winding, lonesome, dangerous, leading to the most amazing view. May your mountains rise into and above the clouds. (Abbey)

I have an invisible connection and a passionate fire in my soul for the Mountain West:

Wilderness Dreams[*]

I came West like a pioneer
Leaving everything but my fear behind.
I had been here many years before
As a child I loved the mountains
From the high country to the desert floor.

They are near the Source of our existence
The birth of the mighty rivers
Is here in the mountain streams.
I remember, I remember
But are they wilderness dreams?

Lesson 1

The conviction that the outer and the inner, the flesh and the spirit are inevitably bound together may be the sublime discovery in life.

---

[*] Nisbett, *Mountains, Hills, and Prairies.*

Humphries Peak, Arizona

TWO

Going Up

> Going up is madness to those who do not
> climb. To those who do go up, it is spiritual
> and emotional freedom.

My dad was a well-known and well-liked businessman in the Texas Panhandle and, when author Louise George decided to write a book about eleven seasoned leaders from that part of the state, one of the men she chose was dad. Her book is entitled "Some REAL Good Old Boys" and dad was about the furthest thing I can imagine from the stereotypical "good ol' boy."

As Louise writes in her book's intro, "the term 'good old boys' was a compliment to a man's character. It meant he was honest and trustworthy; he kept his word, paid his debts, and you could believe what he said except for an occasional stretching of a good story into a slightly better one." I recommend reading her book of biographies. It would probably be an interruption to your current book reading list.

Dad was the unlikely Scoutmaster of my Troop 42 at Central Methodist Church when I was growing up. Scouting was no interruption in my life, in fact, it added so much meaning and value. It was probably an interruption in Dad's life since he was not an avid outdoorsman. Dad played tennis at Amarillo High, liked to walk and run local road races, and was committed to giving my brother and I the outdoor skills and moral fortitude that Scouting instills.

Dad didn't hunt, fish, or throw axes. He did build character in young men as a dozen of us became Eagle Scouts under his leadership. Once an Eagle, always an Eagle. Whatever negative view you may have of Scouting due to social media, the litigious culture, and a few "bad apples," honorable men and women have been associated with the Scouting movement.

From the staff and leaders at Camp Don Harrington and Philmont Scout Ranch; Banker Ray Koehler who presented the Lon C. McCrory "Scout of the Year Award," to District Scout Executive B. J. Lewis, I am indebted to the those who build character by example. In a world flooded with words, these leaders rose above the idle chatter.

One of my avocations has been public speaking—nurtured by Dad's own experience and his Toastmasters training—and, especially, invitations for me to speak at spiritual retreats usually convened at traditional campgrounds. These opportunities to speak and travel were always combined with a mountain climb or two. My family often accompanied me when possible.

In July 2001 my parents and two of my daughters joined me to drive out to Prescott, Arizona, for one of these week-long camps. My wife never cared for spiritual retreats much; she is usually advancing rather than retreating. She does like mountains and hiking, getting out in nature. Lou Ann is an artist, and she loves to create.

Knowing that our travel west on I-40 would carry the family very close to Humphries Peak just ten miles north of Flagstaff, I planned a hike up Arizona's highest point. We would have only one day for this mountain adventure since I was doing the opening session at the Prescott Camp event.

My eighteen-year-old daughter Mallary, my eighty-three-year-old Dad, and I probably got too late of a start on the Humphries Peak Trail for a summer summit free of the afternoon thunderstorms typical in the San Francisco Peaks. The trail is nine miles roundtrip with 3500 feet of vertical gain. Driving to the Trailhead at 9000 feet from our motel in Flagstaff, the skies were clear, and we were excited to be climbing a state highpoint together.

We hiked and ascended well and reached the saddle at 11,780 feet when the wind changed. Now, there are headwinds and tailwinds and katabatic winds and mountain winds that explode out of thunderclouds. We felt the wind blowing harder and harder on the summit ridge and the storm clouds building. Humphries and the San Francisco Peaks are among the four sacred peaks of the Dine, the People, as the Navajo call themselves. Perhaps the mountain deity or spirit is not pleased with our intrusion?

Pushing on up to about 12,000 feet, we could "taste" the summit which stands at 12,633 feet. Rapidly the lightning, rain, and hailstones began to really pelt the ground above us. With electrical flashes all around, I led us back down as quickly as I could. These storms usually last only a short while but our schedule had no margin in it. My mom and youngest daughter were waiting in Flagstaff for our return and the Retreat would start that evening in Prescott.

I had seen the danger of these mountain storms before, and we were all still getting wet and cold without rain gear. We were so close to the summit! With no large rocks to shelter under, we needed to get to some forest cover lower down the mountain. Mallary desperately wanted to go on up and she was visibly disappointed with my decision. As in life, *there is some madness and uncertainty on the mountain pathway.*

The natural elemental force called wind takes numerous forms which attempt to make it visible. *The wind blows where it wishes, and you can hear the sound it makes, but you do not know where it comes from or where it goes.* You see the evidence of wind: a dust devil crossing a plowed field, a blizzard of blowing snow, a windsock on the airplane hangar. It can be a gentle breeze, a gale force storm, a cooling breath of air on a steamy day, or a stinging edge of particles sandblasting your face.

Some of the highest winds on earth have been recorded on Mount Washington in New Hampshire—231 mph in April 1934. Severe wintry storms with hurricane-force wind occur frequently, even in the summer months. When I climbed Mt. Washington in October 2005, the constant winds were blowing at above 60 mph. I remember crawling on my hands and knees to the summit marker at 6288 feet to keep from being blown off balance. State highpoint #38. Check.

My third climb of Mt. Elbert in Colorado in late September 2012 provides another windy example. My son Shawn and son-in-law Scott took my annual Colorado 14ers trip with me. Solo climbs are important, but most climbs are better shared. Hiking and camping on Day 1 was a great way to adjust to the altitude since all three of us had flown to Denver from our homes at sea level.

After climbing to the summit of the Mount of the Holy Cross (14,005 feet), we moved our camp over to North Elbert TH for our Day 3 climb of Elbert. The weather was overcast, and a storm was threatening. We dressed warm and packed our raingear and proceeded up above the tree line. There we met hikers coming down the Northeast Ridge Trail—some were spooked by the impending storm and others were obviously not dressed properly for a winter blast in September.

We decided to descend a few hundred feet into a stand of trees. As we talked it over, we came to the decision that we had the right gear and the right stuff for a summit attempt. The whiteout snow blew in our face all the way to the top where seven or eight inches of snow had accumulated. The wind was *visible* that day.

The truly unseen aspect of wind can symbolize the spirit of a person or place, a deep inner sense, or some force moving across our being, maybe changing our plans or our direction. We readily recognize the role of *team spirit* in an athletic contest, or the name *Spirit of Saint Louis* referring *to* Lindbergh's Atlantic-crossing airplane, or the *Spirit of Christmas* representing a season of giving or time of hope. Wind moves like a phantom.

On the mountain pathway the spirit occasionally shows up as an intangible and aerial awareness that Someone or Something else is present. Climbing alone and reaching the summit of Andorra's highest mountain peak, Comapedrosa, I sensed an invisible companion. I learned upon returning to my family at the trailhead that my ninety-six-year-old Dad had died in his sleep at home while I was on the mountain. I was not alone. Climbing the mountain pathway releases a spirit of freedom that provides true meaning amidst the winds and constraints of life.

I have an invisible companion in the whistling wind:

In Between the Wind*
Great Spirit I fear that I am the only one out here,
but I am not alone, you've made yourself known . . .
In between the wind.

Great Spirit I fear that I have lost my way,
but this is your zone and you make yourself known . . .
In between the wind.

Lesson 2
Failure is relative on the mountain pathway while learning from it is the true success.

---

* Nisbett, *Mountains, Hills, and Prairies.*

Mt. Whitney, California

Photo by Zeimusu on March 25, 2003
https://commons.wikimedia.org/wiki/File:Mount_Whitney_2003–03–25.jpg

THREE

Going Higher

Going Higher Means Digging Deeper.
Further up and further in.

After trying for several years to get a Mount Whitney hiking permit by lottery in California's John Muir Wilderness, one of my climbing partners Kent Barnard and I were starting to feel some real disappointment. We were doing the same process over and over and expecting different results. Insane, right?

You never want disappointment to become a pattern or habit in your inner person. Failure is never final and repetitive patterns can be broken. Mount Whitney would be my 42nd state highpoint if Lady Luck would just allow our names to be pulled out of the Permit box for 2006! Kent decided to break our pattern, do some more research, and find some options.

There was one alternative to individual permits and that was a group permit owned by one of the licensed and authorized Whitney guide services. Okay, what does that mean? Long story short, it meant that this mountain adventure would change from a 21-mile backpacking trail hike to a Mountaineers Route or East Face vertical climb of the highest mountain in the lower 48 states.

We spent a day brushing up on our rock climbing, rope, and rappelling skills and then began the approach from the Mount Whitney TH to Upper Boy Scout Lake at 11,200 feet. The route above would skirt Iceberg Lake, climb the couloir and gully of Class 4 rock on the Mountaineers Route to the Whitney summit at 14,494 feet.

Here is a piece of our guide's report:

"We left camp at 5:00 am sharp, and as we were approaching Iceberg Lake, the sun rose and cast spectacular alpenglow on Mount Muir and the East Face of Mount Whitney. There was a little snow in the initial couloir, and we were able to climb it easily without the use of crampons, although we had them with us just in case. Ice axes did come in handy in this section. Our team moved fast and efficiently up the couloir's steepest parts, which boded well for the more technical ground lying ahead. When we reached the notch at the top of the first couloir, rather than ascend soft snow and crumbly rock in the gully, we opted to climb a rock rib to climber's right. From that point, it was 3rd and 4th class rock all the way to the summit."

Breaking the hiking pattern challenged us—body, mind, and spirit—providing a real emotional experience for me. The first person I called on top of Mount Whitney was my dad. A few transient tears dripped down my face as I told him what an amazing vertical climb it was!

Our AAI guide Joey had taught me so much that inspired confidence and humility in big mountains. On the second day as we inched along a narrow stretch of rock ledge with a steep precipice below us, Joey said, "Tom, you look a little nervous." I replied that when I looked down it was a long drop. Joey said, "Don't look down. Look where you want to step and don't look where you don't want to step." *I have carried that mountain wisdom with me ever since. Fear is a lack of focus.*

As storm clouds began their midday build-up, our time to descend from the Whitney summit quickly materialized. The skies turned from blue to gray. Rather than rappel nine or ten pitches, we agreed to downclimb the upper section while roped together. The team moved efficiently together, and we soon arrived back at our high camp.

The visible nature of terrain can appear at times steep, level, rocky, vertical. Where do I summon the inner resources to face steeper going? Am I acquiring experience and the skills needed? With the confidence gained on the Mountaineers Route and Whitney climb, I prepared for what would be a solo climb of one of the most technically difficult state highpoints—Granite Peak in Montana in September 2007. It comes up next so I will save the details until Chapter 4.

One summer hiking trip when Dad, Shawn, and I were exploring the Pecos Wilderness in northern New Mexico, two unexpected challenges confronted us in one week. We were very experienced backpackers at this point—confident but not cocky. On one long traverse in the high country, we all got separated from each other. It happened so fast and I felt responsible.

After several hours we reunited and marked the lesson learned: *communicate* with *your climbing partners.* Toward the end of our Pecos adventure, we took a side trail headed in the right direction but ended at a steep and long wall of rock. We had to lower our backpacks down the rocky cliff with some cord and then downclimb slowly about forty feet. *Take a rope and know your knots.*

The invisible elements of terrain—endless ups and downs, false summits, deep chasms—remind us of the unknown. We prefer to know what we are up against in life and to gain knowledge and so gain control. I know, for example, that life has its tough times, its ups and downs, and its share of setbacks and losses. I can be philosophical for a while, but I don't know the future. *The terrain of life is mountainous.* Invisible forces lie beneath the visible. The mountain pathway teaches me to be aware of both.

Sudden fear was the invisible force that confronted me and my climbing partner Kent on Idaho's highest mountain just a few months later. Borah Peak is a very steep climb from top to bottom—5550 feet of ascent in only 3.4 miles. There is no water source on Borah and the steep slopes are covered with dry, loose gravel called "scree."

A knife-edged ridge, known as the Chicken Out Ridge, has a more dangerous slope on the North side and involves Class 3 climbing. There is a notch on the ridge that has steep slopes on both sides and is frequently filled with steep, hard snow. Kent and I summited Borah Peak (12,662 feet) on September 3, 2006.

Fear jumped us on the descent. Near the summit there is a small cliff along the ridge that requires a short pitch of rock climbing. Down climbing we veered off course slightly when all the rock in all directions looked the same. We scrambled down in the wrong direction until we were stopped by sheer cliffs dropping thousands of feet.

I remember yelling up to some climbers who were following us down, "this is not the route"! Our enthusiasm had put us in a very precarious position. We slowly ascended, carefully checking every foot placement, until we discovered the best route off the summit. The true test of climbing skills is in exhibiting the strength to descend the mountain. Face the mountain, face the fear. *Going higher means digging deeper.*

I have an invisible agency for mountain and wilderness terrain:

> **Alaska**[*]
> Well, these are the mountains
> And they are my home
> They shelter the elk and the deer
> With dollars in your eyes
> Some developer's disguise,
> Your money is not welcome here.
>
> Now listen you miners and lumbermen too
> Listen you men that build roads.
> My grandfather spoke of a time
> Before fences, of endless forests and trees.
> We've got to have wilderness.
> If we want to be free.

[*] Nisbett, *Mountains, Hills, and Prairies.*

Lesson 3
Climbers tend to be goal-oriented
and relentlessly optimistic, merging flesh
and spirit.

Granite Peak, Montana

Photo taken by jfisher2167 on August 21, 2011
https://commons.wikimedia.org/wiki/File:Granite_Peak_Montana_2.jpg

FOUR

Going Solo

---

*Going solo is a highly developed capacity for
adventure. (Loneliness is the pain of being
alone. Solitude is the purpose of being alone.
Renewal is the power from being alone.)*

Granite Peak in Montana was not intended to be a solo climb for me. It is generally recognized as the most challenging technical climb of the fifty state highpoints. Good climbers have fallen and required rescue. In August 1987, when less than a hundred vertical feet from the summit, a climber fell and seriously injured his right knee, requiring a helicopter rescue by the Sky Top Rescue Service.

To climb the peak "requires good rock-climbing skills, including the technical capability to belay and rappel" which requires two people, trusted partners. Weather in the Montana backcountry can be treacherous with thunderstorms, snow, and freezing conditions at any time of year. "Granite Peak is a great climb, but the weather can be horrible" (Don Jacobs).

My climbing partner Kent had to "bail" on this trip and none of my few trusted climbing partners could make the trip on short notice. My flights were booked. I would explore the Absaroka-Beartooth Wilderness alone. My flight from Little Rock to Billings was easy enough. After arriving, I bought some supplies locally and drove to the trailhead which is about 28 miles west of Red Lodge.

I found a level spot to pitch my tent the first night just off the Silver Lake Trail near Mystic Lake. As I was heating water for breakfast oatmeal and coffee the first morning, a hiker from Billings named Curt introduced himself and asked if we could hike together after I broke camp and caught up with him. "Sure," I said. He would wait for me at the top of the Phantom Creek Trail switchbacks on the saddle ridge to the Froze-To-Death (FTD) Plateau.

So many thoughts had been rolling around in my head as I made the trip to Montana. A young man from our town in Arkansas loved flying and had just completed his solo test for his private license at age 18. The first solo flight of a new pilot includes a takeoff, a short flight, and a safe landing. Flying such a flight is a milestone known as "soloing." A solo pilot must not only be able to fly and navigate the machine in a competent manner, but he also must be able to cope with unpredictable events like mechanical failure and bad weather on their own. Those ideas were what the word "solo" suggested. *Reminder: going solo is a highly developed capacity for adventure.*

I caught up with Curt before we reached the saddle marking the beginning of the Froze-to-Death Plateau and so we hiked and got acquainted. He had a wife and daughter and worked for a Banking company in Billings. I told him about my family.

We visited as we crossed five miles of rocks, boulders, and alpine marshes with only a faint trail at times. Over long periods of time, water and ice have etched the massive peaks, created rock-strewn plateaus and glaciated U-shaped valleys, and gemlike lakes that characterize the Absaroka-Beartooth Wilderness.

I had covered my face with sunscreen for the FTD plateau section and the combination of sun and wind created a mystery condition in my vision. I thought I had snow blindness, but it was not snowing. As the sun melted my sunscreen, the high wind was blowing the thinned lotion into my eyes, and they were burning intensely. Due to a childhood rock fight in our neighborhood trenches, I have practically no vision in my left eye due to that accident. Note: no sunscreen anywhere close to the eyes here. Wind exerts a wicked force.

We reached the three-foot tall, three-sided rock shelters at Tempest Mountain (12,000 feet) at about 5:00 pm and set-up our tents in a steady wind. I was physically tired, so I crawled into my tent home to rest. The tents would rattle all night from the relentless winds requiring more rocks dragged inside through the night to hold them down. "Tempest" is well-named.

The natural elements of earth (dirt, soil, rocks) provide beauty, firm ground to stand on, and living landscapes visible to us. The earth is our home and the land our heritage. One of our best backpacking adventures was a three-week geology trip to the Tetons in Wyoming. Lou Ann and I had been married less than a year and we signed up for this college course led by our professor-friend, Herb Hudgins. This earthy expedition is one we treasure.

My wife and I like to get our hands in the dirt. From fresh, nutrient-rich soil to the thin layers of sand on our rocky hillside homestead, we try to grow things—flowers, vegetables, ground cover. When people lose touch with nature, they often experience isolation and loneliness. On the mountain pathway, rocky terrain provides the firm foundation for exploration and personal growth.

Back to my Montana story, Granite Peak was clearly visible the next morning about one mile distant as Curt and I left our tent shelters about 7:00 am and descended to the East Ridge connecting the two mountains. We climbed up the East Ridge, crossed over the feature called the Snowbridge, and scrambled up three chimneys to the V-notch.

This vertical section made Curt nervous and since he had promised his wife that he would return home, he said he could go no further. I was free to solo the upper section. *This is what I came for.*

The invisible elements of the earth lie beneath what we can easily see—the root structure of trees, the microscopic world of the soil and rocks, the caves and burrows that are home to the wildlife that live there. Often, we *contend* with earth forces like quakes, volcanic eruptions, avalanches, and other violent acts of nature even as they threaten human life. We are *content* with invisible forces like *the* root systems, wildlife species, and microorganisms, that support life.

When I climb in the mountains, I am more aware of and dependent on this inter-connectedness. This awareness penetrates my own subterranean topography, uniting my conscious and subconscious thoughts with the terrain, merging visible and invisible. John Muir exulted in a sense of oneness with the rock. *I needed to do the same.*

Curt had decided to sit and wait so I decided to climb around to the steeper wall where some Class 5 rock guarded the summit. Above the V-notch the route ascends through ledges, cracks, gullies, cliffs, and chimneys where hands, legs, back, and your whole body are useful. In addition, good route-finding skills are needed to navigate successfully this section.

The goal then is to reach the "keyhole" on the ridge above. From about 15 feet below the keyhole, I climbed up a chute to the left of the keyhole to the top of the ridge and then scrambled on the west side of the ridge to the summit.

Guided climbing leads to a guided mentality. Solo climbing builds self-reliance. *Going alone is a developed capacity for adventure, navigating the visible and the invisible, combining the intuitive work of the soul with conscious reasoning.*

The downclimb was intimidating without a partner and ropes for rappelling. Descending the ridge to the keyhole, I proceeded slowly approaching the enormous matrix of ledges, rock faces, cliffs, and vertical chutes. I was excited to be soloing but very cautious until I reached Curt just past the V-notch. We hiked back down to our high camp at Tempest Mountain by 2:30 pm. With no appetite for eating, I drank a little beef broth after resting and re-packing.

We broke camp around 4:30 pm and began the five-mile hike back across the FTD Plateau as evening and darkness came on us quickly. Route-finding was difficult and we had trouble locating the right canyon off the Plateau to the switchbacks. It was after 7:30 pm when we began descending three more miles toward Mystic Lake.

The last two hours required our headlamps as we hiked in the dark feeling fatigued and dehydrated. We found the campsite around 9:30 pm where I had left some extra gear and collapsed on the ground and slept without tents. It was a clear sky with a million stars and cold temps all night. I finally fell asleep thinking about my 47th state highpoint on my first attempt!

The next morning, we hiked three miles out to the Mystic Lake parking area. Curt invited me to his home for a steak dinner with his family and an overnight stay before my flight the following day. It was good to have a climbing companion **and** to solo the upper section of Granite Peak. *I am feeling renewed by companionship and independence.*

I have an unseen link within myself to mountainous terrain and the people who were here before me:

Blue Lake*

I remember the southwest American
Indian people of the pueblos and the plains
Is this all that remains
Just a mountain reservation?

Take me back to Taos New Mexico
Among the white-barked aspen trees,
Up to Blue Lake please
It is this soul's alpine destination.

Lesson 4
There is a deep connection between the seen and the unseen, the visible and the invisible. Find the courage to go alone at special times.

---

* Nisbett, *Mountains, Hills, and Prairies.*

Mt. Shasta, California
Aerial photo of Mount Shasta taken by Ewen Denney on June 22, 2006
https://en.wikipedia.org/wiki/Mount_Shasta#/media/File:MtShasta_aerial.JPG

FIVE

Going Alone

---

*Going alone can also produce a hard-won
grace. An internal dialogue characterizes
mountain climbers and trail-runners.*

Following a week-long spiritual retreat north of Santa Cruz near
Boulder Creek, California, at the Redwood Christian Camp, I
drove my rental car to I-5. Californians call their major highways
by their numbers: The 5, the 99, the 101—So I took "The 5" toward
Sacramento and on to the northern towns of Dunsmuir and Shasta
at the foot of the mountain. It was the national holiday celebrating
independence and I had planned an independent solo climb of Mt.
Shasta (14,179 ft.) in the Cascades.

After my mountaintop experience and spiritual high from
Redwood Camp, I was ready to put my feet on the snowy mountain and ascend as the "climbing companion of Christ." Eugene
Peterson uses this expression in the Sermon on the Mountain from
his translation, The Message.

I had not invited anyone else to join me on this adventure
as I wanted to test the alpine skills I was learning and enjoy being

alone. I stayed overnight at the Dunsmuir Inn which was owned and operated by a family from Bihar State in India. We had a pleasant visit, talked about my trips to India, and learned that their uncle owned the Sands Motel in my hometown of Dalhart, Texas. *Everyone has a connection to Dalhart . . .*

On the morning of the Fourth, I drove up to the Bunny Flat TH at 6900 feet. I registered and paid for the $20 wilderness permit and began to lighten my backpack and re-pack due to the very warm temps. I departed the BFTH around 10:30 am and climbed up by the Sierra Club Hut at Horse Farm near 8000 feet easily by 11:00 am and on to the 50/50 flat area just below the snow line.

After a lunch snack, I put on my crampons and continued to climb up to Lake Helen at 10,400 feet by 2:15 pm. If there is a lake it was snow-covered but there was a narrow rock outcropping or moraine for a few tents. It was so warm that I had no tent but just used my bivy bag and Thermarest pad. There were 100s if not 1000s of monarch butterflies filling the afternoon skies above the Lake Helen feature. I fell asleep around 9:00 pm after viewing fireworks filling the night sky way down the mountain near Lake Siskiyou. *Freedom in the hills!*

The visible natural elements of snow and ice, fresh powder, melting snow, and glaciers are why I love climbing in the Cascades—Shasta, Hood, Rainier, Baker. Mt. Shasta is a potentially active stratavolcano in the Cascade Volcanic Arc. There are seven named glaciers on Mt. Shasta—Whitney Glacier is the longest and the Hotlum Glacier is the most voluminous glacier in the state of California.

Snow and glacial travel require some alpine training, mountaineering skills, and climbing gear with at least crampons and ice axe. Your eyes (and your feet) quickly tell you that this is an unstable terrain.

I awoke on July 5th at 3:40 am and noticed 5–6 people with headlamps lit already scattered up the mountain. The moon was full but was setting in the west almost blood red in color. I layered up, attached my crampons, put on my helmet with headlamp, grabbed my ice axe and started climbing at 4:00 am. I made the top of the Red Banks and the left chute through the crux by 7:30 am. This is the most technical section of the route as the chutes are full of snow and ice, very steep, and top out at around 13,000 ft.

The route then heads up Misery Hill where I had to dig deep to summon the will to keep going alone. Mountains and obstacles in life –anything that makes progress, movement, or achieving goals more difficult—teach us to explore the deeper regions of our soul. Attacking the switchbacks and the upper snow fields of Avalanche Gulch, I stepped on the rocky summit at 14,179 feet arriving about 9:20 am. It was a clear, bluebird day but windy and cool on the upper mountain and the summit.

The invisible elements in nature beneath snow and ice include unseen dangers of hidden blue ice, winter's frozen indifference, and deep crevasses. Up here what you can't or don't see can kill you. Some invisible forces surprise, startle, or set us back. Some threaten our lives. Pray with eyes open for good luck.

Every year climbers die on Mt. Hood in the Cascades when invisible or unexpected forces like whiteout blizzards or rapidly moving weather systems slam them. Mt. Hood can create its own weather and be a nasty little mountain even though it rises to only 11,239 feet. Two climbing partners and I were blinded by a whiteout at the top of the Palmer Glacier in June 2007.

Most climbing injuries and deaths on Mt. Hood have occurred when inexperienced or ill-equipped climbers were hit by falling rock, ice, or snow; or fell on steep slopes or into crevasses; or became disoriented in poor weather conditions. *Adapt when things change. The mountain will still be there.*

Mountain climbing clearly involves issues like weather, known and unknown risks, safety, and security. Climbing in South America five years ago, we met a TSA agent who was climbing Aconcagua alone and failed to assess changing conditions on the mountain. He seemed to have "checked the boxes and gear lists" hoping to summit a big mountain, void of critical thinking and alpine skills. In mountain climbing, those omissions will get you in *trouble.*

In 2019, I drove my rental car from Sydney over the Great Dividing Range toward the town of Jindabyne and on to Thredbo which is a snow-skiing village in the Kosciuszko National Park in the Main Range of the Snowy Mountains. Mt. Kosciuszko is mainland Australia's highest mountain. The trail was dirt and snow and was an easy seven mile walk to the summit and back. I did get a late start that day, the Thredbo Chairlift on the lower slopes closed late afternoon, and I was chasing the sunset, while the ski patrol was chasing me . . . at times invisibly.

Back on Shasta's summit, I ate a piece of granola bar and drank some water before leaving the top at 9:35 am. On the descent I met four or five roped groups being guided up by Shasta Mountain Guides (SMG) or other guiding services. I was soloing this climb which required skills I did not have only a few years earlier. I better concentrate, I thought, I'm not down yet.

One hour off the top and I reached the Crux—the chute through the Red Banks. I glissaded on my butt down the steep section below for thirty minutes because others before me had left a good trough. I was aware of the possibility of going too fast, losing control, or snagging a crampon in the trough and wrenching a knee. Focus.

I arrived back at my Lake Helen camp at 11:35 am. I slept for two hours, packed up, and hiked on down to Horse Camp hut and on out to the TH by 3:30 pm. Writing this account makes the descent sound easy. The actual descent required lots of focus and attention. *It was a hard-won grace. This "hard-won grace" is something like honor or favor held inside, in the deeper regions of the soul. External reward or public praise is absent.*

I have this hidden DNA with Snowy Mountains:

The Land of Enchantment[*]
The sun danced across the meadow,
Early in the late spring
After the winter snows
Had melted and flowed
Clearing the morning of its cold.

---

[*] Nisbett, *Mountains, Hills, and Prairies.*

Lesson 5
The motivating characteristics of a
mountaineer include a high pain threshold
and meticulous self-improvement.
Test your skills.

Montserrat, Spain

Photo taken by Josep Renalias
https://en.wikipedia.org/wiki/Montserrat_(mountain)#/media/File:Montserrat_des_de_
Manresa.JPG

SIX

Going Near

Going near is not simply passing through, but
is living on the edge, seeking the thin places.

Driving from Barcelona, Spain, to Andorra la Vella, Andorra, in May 2014, to climb the highest mountain there, we discovered that we were going right by the Benedictine abbey of Santa Maria de Montserrat which is located high on the mountain. The monastery was founded in the 11th century and rebuilt between the 19th and 20th centuries. Miles of trails circle the mountain and ascend its highest craggy summits. Everything from the mountain's natural beauty to the structures carved out of the sedimentary rock is breathtaking.

What great fortune to go near!

Our daughter Savanah and her husband Scott were living in Barcelona doing some graduate work and they helped arrange the Andorra climb. I have never hiked the 500-mile Camino de Santiago (The Way of St. James) but friends who have say that it is an awesome experience meeting so many fellow hikers and pilgrims. I hoped to meet fellow mountain climbers on this trip.

I have hiked the highpoints in Spain's Canary Islands in 2014 as well as Portugal's highpoint and Portugal's Azores islands in 2013. My friend and climbing partner Kent and his wife Linda lived on the outskirts of Lisbon for a couple of years. We took flights out to the Azores and met for two days of hiking and climbing on Pico Island.

Mount Pico is a currently quiet stratavolcano located on Pico Island in the mid-Atlantic archipelago of the Azores. It is the highest mountain of Portugal at 7713 feet above sea level and its park is a designated nature reserve. We walked about 4 miles on the Saturday we arrived in Madalena. We explored and immersed ourselves in the local culture attending a wedding and a feast where all were welcome.

We climbed Mount Pico on Sunday covering about ten kilometers roundtrip—the route being described as a Class 2 scramble. We agreed that the experience was a steep and strenuous climb and that "two persons make a shorter road."

Back to our story, there were four of us in Spain and Andorra in May 2014 creating memories and getting a broader sense of history by driving to new places and unexpected adventures. Montserrat literally means "serrated mountain" (like the common handsaw). That describes its peculiar aspect with a multitude of rock formations that are visible from a great distance. The mountain is made up of strikingly pink conglomerate, a form of sedimentary rock. Montserrat has been of religious significance since pre-Christian times, when the Romans built a temple to honor the Roman goddess, Venus.

The highest summit of Montserrat is called *Sant Jeroni* (Saint Jerome) and stands at 4055 feet asl. It is accessible by hiking trails which connect from the top entrance to the monastery or the base of the mountain. Montserrat is part of the GR footpath 172 and the Cavall Bernat at 3645 feet is an important rock feature popular with climbers. The *Gran Recorridos (GR) is* a network of long-distance footpaths in Europe, mostly in France, Belgium, the Netherlands, and Spain.

We spent as much time as we could and lingered in Montserrat—walking the grounds and hiking a few of the many trails. I remember thinking "this feels like a pilgrimage." My conversion story is published and available and so I want to describe, instead, some stages of my spiritual journey.

U2 has a song from the *No Line on the Horizon* album that is entitled "Moment of Surrender." According to Jonas Steverud:

> *The moment of surrender is THE moment of realization of what we have and are doing to ourselves AND turning that over to some other authority—much like 12 step programs.*

My spiritual pilgrimage began with surrender, taking one step to freedom in Christ followed by many ascending steps to living free. Fifteen of the Psalms, 120–134, carry the title of "A Song of Ascents." They are variously called Gradual Psalms, Songs of Steps, or Pilgrim Songs. Many scholars believe the title indicates that these psalms were sung by worshippers as they ascended the road to Jerusalem to attend three pilgrim festivals. More than half of these songs are cheerful, and all of them are hopeful. *I sing because I'm happy, I sing because I'm free.*

A Celtic Christian rock band called Iona has an album entitled *Open Sky* with a tune "Songs of Ascent" that includes these words:

> *My soul is awakened, with truth to astound me.*
> *An emptiness for You to fill*
> *My soul a cavern for Your sea.*

When I came to Jesus in October 1974, I didn't come to a set of beliefs, I came to a Person. My surrender of everything to God came later during a crisis over finances in July 1980, although my mom would say that after several miscarriages, she prayed for a healthy baby boy and dedicated me to God even before I was born. I grew up in church and attended Family Camp every summer as I've said. Life can easily take you down some wrong paths and result in a series of poor decisions leading to an empty soul. Some things we do to ourselves, and some things are done to us.

My perspective has been then and ever since that surrender to God is not the sadness of defeat but the surety of victory. We do not truly live *for* victory but *from* victory: *An emptiness for God to fill. Let God fill your heart with hopeful songs.*

The visible natural phenomenon that we call "sky" can be deep blue and clear, filled with cirrus or cumulus clouds, or foggy and overcast. In the high country and vast wilderness areas, the sky is bigger! (Montana isn't called Big Sky country for no reason!) On a clear day in the mountains, you can tell the approximate time of day by the sun or read the constellations to navigate by the stars on a clear night. Knowing the type of clouds in the sky enables you to understand and even predict the weather. *The sky is your ally.*

This musical poetry from Family Camp is hidden in my subconscious where so many ideas were sung into memory:

> *For the beauty of the earth,*
> *For the glory of the skies,*
> *For the love which from our birth*
> *Over and around us lies.*
> *(Pierpoint)*

The invisible aspects of the sky like heaven, distant galaxies, and "the realm above" are things we cannot help but wonder about when we are in the high country. Sometimes that reflection brings a quiet peace and other times endless sky, and infinite space is disconcerting. Is there life out there? Where is heaven? Is there an afterlife in the vastness of the universe? I wrote these verses in the wilderness:

Nature Is your Life's Sanctuary*
Nature is your life's sanctuary, try
Anticipating movement in the sky,
The miracle of life
Swiftly passing by
Silver-slivered moon
Nightly on its flight.

Constellations ponder on everlasting life
Mankind's infidelity cuts like a knife
Nature is your life's sanctuary, try
Listening to her speak, sigh
The miracle of life swiftly passing by.

---

* Nisbett, *Mountains, Hills, and Prairies.*

Every quest begins with a question. I have found many of the answers and my spiritual journey has, like mountain paths, had its ascents and descents, its peaks and valleys, its ups and downs. John Eldredge writes that *Walking with God* begins with and continues to be a process of learning to hear the voice of God; finding our way back to joy; enduring seasons of struggle to experience break-through; discovering God in our losses; and recovering hope and the desire to find new beginnings. *These patterns I have learned to recognize and to realize that for me the mountain pathway is like therapy for the wounded soul.*

I keep a written record of sacred times "when God called" in my life—the holy whisper of God prompting me to action. In most instances God used a person to speak through as a personal invitation to a deeper life. From October 1974 when God spoke through a guest preacher's invitation to follow Christ, many times God has spoken through another human: a phone call to serve on an International Board in 1989; a personal request to teach a Law School Bible Study; a phone message when I was teaching in Spain offering a new university position; a lunch invitation from a local doctor to raise money for an eye clinic in Kenya; a call to speak to a national group in Canada; a friend's invitation to teach in India; another similar call to do training in Kenya; a meeting with a development colleague to plant a new church; and an email from a friend to lead a men's small group. I value a sense of mystery and of childlike wonder:

> *For the wonder of each hour,*
> *Of the day and of the night,*
> *Hill and vale, and tree and flower,*
> *Sun and moon, and stars of light.*
> *(Pierpoint)*

Lesson 6
You don't know who you are until you know Whose you are. There are many voices in the city but there is One voice on the mountain.

Comapedrosa, Andorra

SEVEN

Going Together

Going together is more than a notion of going with someone or attending an event, rather it is a community moving and journeying together.

O ur trip to Europe in May 2014, particularly Spain and Andorra, was characterized by excellent weather with occasional soft rain. Our daughter Savanah and her husband Scott were living in Barcelona and working there. My wife and I just had to visit and so we pitched the idea of a weekend trip to climb Comapedrosa and see the small country of Andorra.

The drive was mostly in a northerly direction and the scenery was spectacular! We just had to take a short side trip to the Montserrat mountain range in Spain because it was so near our route. It was an unexpected highlight of the weekend journey and would take on a special spiritual meaning. We arrived at the Andorra border crossing, showed our passports, and drove on into the quaint and captivating capital city of Andorra la Vella.

We checked into the Anyos Park Mountain and Wellness Resort in La Massana, one of the seven parishes of the Principality of Andorra where we had lodging reserved for a few nights. The Resort had a great gym, pool, and spa and was within walking distance of shops and restaurants. We walked two to three miles and explored this mountain town. *Wellness and Mountains go together!*

Early the next morning Scott and I headed for the trailhead at Arinsal, another one of the seven parishes of Andorra, and started up the mountain. I remember it was a little cold at first, but it warmed up as the sun got higher in the sky on a bluebird day, perfect weather for climbing an unfamiliar snow-covered mountain.

Scott climbed with me while there was no snow on the lower trails, and we reached a closed ski lodge structure after a couple of hours. He turned back there because he had worn the wrong shoes for snow-covered trails. Scott would love this mountain in winter because he loves snow skiing. He reminds me of my 20-something self!

I wore my dependable Asolo alpine boots and continued in the snow all the way to the top of this snowy mountain. In 1946 the Zanatta family started making boots in a little shop in Nervesa della Battaglia, Italy. The family business grew after the Second World War and really flourished in the 1960s and 1970s as the second generation of the Zanatta family continued the values of their parents. The Asolo brand was founded in 1975 by Giancarlo Tanzi who invented the first trekking boots using Cordura materials and he launched Gore-Tex lined footwear. The third generation Zanatta family bought the Asolo brand in 1998.

I reached the summit of the 9656-foot snow-covered Comapedrosa before noon and went back down by 2:00 pm with a roundtrip time of seven hours. Coming down the mountain easily from Comapedrosa's summit I had plenty of time to think. I thought about my lifelong love of the mountains, the crisp mountain air, clear water in its creeks and rivers, and its deep snow.

Water, in its frozen or liquid form, is one of the visible elements necessary for life and survival in the mountains. I've carried plenty of water backpacking in the dry Big Bend National Park of

Texas and in the Lost River Range of Idaho. Give me mountains with glaciers and streams!

Melting snow for hot water on our glacial climbs and camps demonstrates water's essential nature and the human body's need for hydration. Graduating to a Katadyn water filtering system and HydraPak bladder eliminated our need to carry so many water containers, and reduced time spent boiling and treating suspect water. Water is life!

Love of the mountains is a core value of mine, and it is a family value. Wallace Stegner, American novelist and environmentalist—who was often called "The Dean of Western Writers"—used this expression: "Retreat upward!" To me, that means: *Go to the mountains!*

Returning from the top of Comapedrosa, I saw Scott waiting at the Trailhead. Lou Ann and Savanah were close by having pizza for lunch at Surf Arinsal, a local restaurant serving Argentinean cuisine. My brother Rick had called from Arkansas while I was on the mountain and relayed the news that my dad had died peacefully in his sleep late Friday night. That was our Saturday morning and I had felt Dad's presence with me several times on the mountain. *I was not alone.*

Dad had celebrated his 96th birthday just eight days earlier and privately we had talked about the mountain. He told me how much he loved me and my family and the great relationships and many adventures we had together. We hiked and climbed many mountains on our life-journey. Dad showed us how to live and he showed us how to die. *This summit is for you Dad!*

That evening while the girls visited and Scott watched a soccer championship game between *Real Madrid and Atletico de Madrid,* I planned Dad's memorial service knowing his favorite Bible verses and Christian hymns. I knew we would sing *How Great Thou Art* which includes the memorable stanza "When I look down from lofty mountain grandeur and hear the brook and feel the gentle breeze." I also knew that I would speak on the scriptures that say, "I have fought the good fight, I have finished the race, I have kept the faith." *Dad was part of the Greatest Generation who genuinely demonstrated a life force or Spirit strength.*

The invisible aspects of water surprise us: when I look at another person I do not think: "their physical body is almost 70% water." But it is. It needs constant hydration. Sometimes we do not recognize the faint signal called "thirst" until our throats are dry and our body weak. Water also represents a concealed *life force* like *breath* or *blood,* not always in our conscious thoughts but so essential to a living soul.

On Sunday morning we began our return drive to Barcelona. We stopped along the mountain road at Organya, walked through a shop or two, and bought an espresso. The views were inspiring. These are vistas that clear the heart of earthly sorrow and lead the soul up to its best and highest sources. (Bowles) As we traveled, we could view "Saw Mountain" in the distance and the memories of Santa Maria de Montserrat, and its peaceful cloister watered my soul. *We are a community moving together.*

Scott and I have formed a great son-in-law and father-in-law relationship through hiking and climbing. In April 2012, Scott, Savanah, and I climbed Ireland's highest mountain, Carrauntoohil, on a windy and snowy day. That experience created a mutual desire to do the Three Peaks Challenge in Wales, England, and Scotland. During a rainy week in September 2017, we successfully completed Mt. Snowdon, Scafell Pike, and Ben Nevis together.

On the summit of Ben Nevis, two Scotsmen asked where we were from and we replied "Texas," hoping to impress them. One Scot pulled out his flask of his single malt whiskey and offered us a swig. He then turned to the other Scot and asked, "Do ya think it's time to sacrifice the Texans?" That was our cue to bid them "mar sin leat" and descend from those mountains.

Comapedrosa and Montserrat had been an unexpected blessing far from my own Ozark home-base. Sensing dad's presence on the snowy section to the Comapedrosa summit and processing so many memories after receiving the news of dad's quiet passing, cleared my heart of earthly sorrow. Mountain summits and expansive vistas give valuable perspective.

I have a direct current connecting me to my dad's love of mountains:

Father Sky (Son's Prayer)[*]
Father Sky
Teach us to fly
To reach high
To laugh and cry
Deep blue eyes
By day
Sparkle white
By night
Hold us close
To Mother Earth
And waltz with us
Across the universe

Lesson 7
Mountain pathways draw us into a sense of retreating distance, toward a mystery not yet seen, on a journey with trusted friends.

---

[*] Nisbett, *Mountains, Hills, and Prairies.*

Wheeler Peak, New Mexico

Photo taken by Davishan99

https://commons.wikimedia.org/wiki/File:Wheeler_Peak,_NM.JPG

EIGHT

Going Above and Beyond

---

*Going Above and Beyond means more than
doing an excellent job. It means the season
of continuous effort becomes effortless.
You find the flow.*

My brother Rick and I knew that both mom and dad wanted their bodies cremated after their physical death. They had talked it over and made sure we knew their wishes. *The soul lives on.* Scattering or interring their dust-like remains would be up to us.

Mom preferred her "dust to dust" dispersion in some central Texas bluebonnet field in the April bloom. She loved blue and owned several paintings of bluebonnets. Dad's choice would be for the eternal wind to distribute his ashes far and wide when released from a mountain summit.

After dad's gentle passing in May 2014 at the age of ninety-six, we began to plan a late August trip to Wheeler Peak in New Mexico for the above and beyond experience. My brother Rick and I met in Waco, Texas, and drove over to dad's birthplace in Stephenville. No trace of Dad. We traveled on to Amarillo where dad graduated from high school and lived late in life from age 78 to age 90. We walked two miles at Paramount Park like we had done with dad many times over twelve years. He seemed very present though memory is a strong spirit.

After driving from Amarillo to the Taos Ski Valley the next day, Rick and I hiked two miles up to Williams Lake at about 10,000 feet elevation to set-up camp. The next morning Rick encouraged me to go on alone as the altitude was still affecting him. I left Williams Lake at 6:30 am and found the climbers' trail #62 to the summit which I reached at 8:10 am.

Spending about 20 minutes on top, I thought about our previous summits of Wheeler. One of our first attempts missed Wheeler's summit when Dad and I mistook Mt. Walter (13,133) for Wheeler Peak (13,161). We went back the next year to correct the mistake and signed the logbook in the metal summit register on Wheeler Peak.

On my winter climb of Wheeler in 2016, Williams Lake was covered with ice and snow and on the slopes above there I was "post-holing" through waist-deep snow. My new climber-friend Jorge who introduced himself on the trail back to Taos Ski Valley and I grabbed some lunch at the Stray Dog Cafe. Further down the mountain, Red Willow Creek was flowing through the Taos Pueblo. *I love this mountain!*

I've had encounters with summer thunderstorms on Wheeler, climbed to the summit on winter snow, and helped my daughter Candace carry my two-year old grandson to the top in August 2008. In August 2014 I stood alone reflecting on this sacred mountain and then watching as the wind quickly whisked dad's ashes away . . . ashes to ashes, dust to dust. *His soul lives on.*

This almost but not quite visible aspect on the mountain pathway is called "spirit" and it reveals itself as willpower or team effort. It is intangible but it touches the tangible. It is detected as desire and joie de vivre. It is the joy of living in the struggle, joy in the steep climb, joy in the suffering, joy in the weary descent from the heights. It is the joy of a *spirited* climbing partner.

I descended to Williams Lake at 9:40 am and reunited with Rick giving him a full account of the silent ceremony on top.

Thankful for the solitude, nevertheless, I wish that Rick had felt up to reaching the summit. There is something in C.S. Lewis' THE LAST BATTLE from the Chronicles of Narnia about going "further up and further in." I went to the edge on that bluebird morning and I'm glad I did. It is one of the thin places for me.

There are truly invisible elements on the mountain pathway: soul or essence or being. Those words are interchangeable. *Learning to read the visible elements or facets of mountains helps us to identify the invisible forces with which we contend, inevitably bound together. We are reaching for the essential.*

The "dark night of the soul" OR the identity crisis of who we are OR the loss of our essential nature are valley or pit places. Identify those issues before embarking on the mountain pathway because this is no place for delicate souls. *The mountain pathway doesn't make you who you are, it reveals who you are.*

I have a traceable thread running through the high-country freedom:

Thunderbird[*]

My heart's in the highlands
Where the wildlife live free
The mountains are my woman,
She's been calling to me.

Sing to me thunderbird
You stir the heavens with light
Reveal to me your mystery
Your secrets of life

Lesson 8
Climbing teaches that you can do hard things: hard things mean not giving up; not giving up lifts your spirit, which gives you hope. That is going above and beyond.

---

[*] Nisbett, *Mountains, Hills, and Prairies.*

Mt. Harvard, Colorado

https://www.14ers.com/peaks/10003/mount-harvard

NINE

Going Full Circle

---

*Going Full Circle brings you home where your
heart is. There you find your true self.*

I had breakfast in Buena Vista, Colorado, at the Evergreen Cafe on the outside deck in September 2014. It was still cloudy and overcast after raining through the night. I had eggs, bacon, and pancakes plus lots of coffee. *Let's drink some coffee and get after it!*

Back at the cabin where I had been sitting out the monsoon rains after successful climbs of Mt. Yale and Mt. Princeton, I looked toward Mt. Harvard and there was a rainbow in the clouds and mist! *I hope the weather will permit me to climb Harvard tomorrow.* With the snow likely up high, I will have to see the Columbia traverse before I commit to the Harvard-Columbia combination.

Just a year earlier Shawn and I had climbed nine 14ers in a week on our annual Colorado trip and had started number 10 on Mt. Harvard when one of my leg muscles locked down. I returned in 2014 to this *unfinished business* called Harvard. While I waited for better weather, I walked and hiked the Barbara Whipple Trail into the Midland Hills in Buena Vista east of the Arkansas River. I covered over four miles at 8000 feet and stretched out tight muscles.

I found a print shop in town and made copies of the Mt. Harvard-Columbia traverse before driving up to the North Cottonwood Creek Trailhead. Steady rain still filled the high country. There was only one other car in the parking lot when I arrived late afternoon. A few minutes later a woman and her small white dog emerged from the trail, wet and weary, and drove away.

I hiked one mile up the trail and back at the 10,000 feet elevation returning soaking wet. I took off my wet clothes and slept in the truck as everything outside was soaked and light rain continued. I made some mac and cheese hoping the skies would clear before morning.

Night is a natural but ominous element that takes on a different significance on the mountain pathway. Of course, on a rainy, overcast night when it is particularly dark, shrouded in mystery, and rest is your only option, you are unable to see much. *To know a mountain, you must sleep upon it.* (Longstaff)

I have grown to consider night as a friend in the backcountry and wild places. Your eyes adjust to the dark and your soul enlarges when the clear nights reveal a billion stars all around. Hiking and climbing at night exact a certain humility and self-awareness while they enhance your physical health and spiritual well-being.

The Mount Harvard climb in the Collegiate Peaks Wilderness of the San Isabel National Forest is 12.6 miles roundtrip . . . 13 miles with a short side trip to Bear Lake. The vertical gain is 4550 feet. I left the North Cottonwood Creek Trailhead around 6:00 am behind two hunters who had permits for bighorn sheep. After visiting with them just past the footbridge, I quickly climbed out of the river valley and put as much distance as I could between us. I never saw them nor any other hikers all day after leaving the trailhead area.

Most of the real dangers in the high country are obviously weather (blue sky lightning) and wild animals (encounters are rare). I watch out for hunters and weird people, but they are scarce in the higher elevations and mountain summits.

Night and darkness do conjure up fears, uncertainties, and suppressed emotions. They are some of the invisible elements we face in all places—high and low. They are usually part of the *unfinished business* in our lives—unresolved conflicts, broken relationships, and restless souls—real but smaller when faced honestly.

My 2014 Harvard climb was like many of my old backpacking climbs—long approach, good trails, visible goal, steep summit pyramid, and rock climbing to the top on big boulders. Snow on the summit. Light overcoming darkness. *What's not to like!*

The climb took me 5.5 hours upward and I was feeling my body aches as I reached the summit. "Climbing shows you that you can do hard things." (Erikka Ols) It was windy and snowy on top, so I stayed only 30 minutes. I descended in 3.5 hours because of the good trails. Studying the Columbia traverse from several points, I decided to save Mt. Columbia for next September. There were icy and slippery conditions on the snowy ridge connecting the two mountains. *It will still be there next year.*

And it was. In late September 2015, I returned to Colorado alone to attempt four more 14ers in the Sawatch Range. Flying this time from Little Rock to the Colorado Springs airport, I rented a Ford 150 truck with four-wheel drive and high clearance. I drove to Buena Vista and directly up to the North Cottonwood TH where I camped last September. I set up camp and did some short hikes to acclimate before dark.

The next morning was the first day of autumn and I left the NC trailhead at 6:30 on the nice trail into Horn Fork Basin. It took me an hour and forty-five minutes to cover the first three miles to reach the Columbia Trail turnoff. The western slopes of Columbia are steep and scree-covered leading to the very rocky summit ridge. I reached the summit at 11:45 am and stayed on top for a few pictures before starting my descent on the ten-mile roundtrip loop. *Columbia had waited for me. The mountains always do.*

Going full circle brings you home. While I genuinely love my home and family in the Ozark Highlands that I call "Base Camp," the Sangre de Cristos and the Rockies formed in my heart a love for mountain terrain. In 2016, our family received word that mom had passed quietly in her sleep at age ninety-eight and a half. We were hiking and climbing in New Zealand that November and had hoped to return home before mom died.

My daughter Savanah and I would find a beautiful Central Texas bluebonnet field for mom's ashes later in the following spring. *After the winter snows had melted and flowed . . . Her soul lives on!*

The circle of life moves us all through despair and hope, through faith and love, 'til we find our place on the path unwinding. Going full circle for me now means retreating upward every year on mountain pathways.

I sense in the mountains an escape from the city and a link to the sacred:

> **Colorado Bound**[*]
> *Me and my old spotted hound*
> *We're headed for a mountain town,*
> *Sweet smell of the spruce and the pine*
> *There are cool nights on our mind,*
> *You're not going to find us around,*
> *We're Colorado Bound.*

Lesson 9
Climbing began as a passion for the mountains and gradually took its place next to family, next to work, next to life. Retreat Upward.

---

* Nisbett, *Mountains, Hills, and Prairies*.

Afterword

For many people in the world, the landscape before us would be foreboding. For us, it had been a gradual ascent from the unknown into the familiar. Beyond the last villages we no longer saw strange human alterings of the scene, but rather the workings of nature common to all the world's alpine areas: glaciers, rivers, clouds, granite, blue sky, raindrops, wildlife, and friends who shared our passions. We were home again.

GALEN ROWELL, EXPEDITION CHRONICLES

When I retreat upward on the mountain pathway, my soul begins to enlarge. The essential nature of who I am becomes clearer, larger. Ascending and descending in the high country, I gain a new perspective above the crowded places below. Can the soul really grow and develop?

Yes, and it can shrink. If the eyes are the window of the soul, then the light from inside a person is visible. I have looked into the empty eyes of boy soldiers in West Africa and the homeless in America and seen nothing, no light. The soul can shrink, and life can kill the spirit of a person. Or *what good is it for someone to gain the whole world, yet forfeit their soul?*

We need pathways for the soul to enlarge and come alive. We also need companions and mentors like my dad to walk with us. I found my pathway in the mountains and high-country wilderness. Find a trailhead and follow the path to the boulders and climb beyond where the path ends. *There you will see the vistas that clear the heart of earthly sorrow and lead the soul up to its highest Source.*

Playlist for the Reader

- Aerial Boundaries—Michael Hedges
- Wedding Rain—Liz Story
- Beyond the Desert—Dave Beegle
- First Ride—Don Ross
- Mile High Country—Michael Gulezian
- Winter Walk—David Nevue
- Rain—Michael Mucklow
- The Most Beautiful Sky—Stephen Bennett
- Ignition—Michael Hedges
- Embryonic Journey—Jefferson Airplane
- A Ripple Effect—Erik Mongrain
- Breakfast in the Field—Michael Hedges
- Planet Blossom—Michael Waters
- Distant Shore—Bobby Wynn
- Lady Bird—Stephen Bennett
- A Life Well Lived—Dave Beegle
- Cloud Forest—Trace Bundy
- Keep It Simple—Tommy Emmanuel
- The Double Planet—Michael Hedges

- The Bright Field—Brooks Williams
- Strawberry Fields Forever—Stephen Bennett
- Shades of Green—Phil Keaggy

Resources for the Reader

Bass, Dick. *Seven Summits.* New York: Warner Books, 1986.

Bernbaum, Edwin. *Sacred Mountains of the World.* Cambridge: Cambridge University Press, 2022.

Chouinard, Yvon. *Let My People Go Surfing: The Education of a Reluctant Businessman.* New York: Penguin Press, 2005.

Egan, Timothy. *The Worst Hard Time.* Boston: Mariner, 2006.

Eldredge, John. *Walking With God.* Nashville: Thomas Nelson, 2016.

Galen Rowell: A Retrospective. San Francisco: Sierra Club, 2006.

George, Louise. *Some REAL Good Old Boys.* Baltimore: Otter Bay, 2010.

Gire, Ken. *The North Face of God: Hope for the Times when God Seems Indifferent.* Tyndale House, 2006.

Holmes, Don W. *Highpoints of the United States.* Salt Lake City: University of Utah Press, 1990.

Louv, Richard. *Last Child in the Woods.* Chapel Hill, NC: Algonquin, 2005.

Nichols, John. *If Mountains Die.* New York City: Knopf Publishers, 1979.

Nisbett, Tom. *Mountains, Hills, and Prairies: A Topography of the Soul.* Self-published, 2006.

Noyce, Wilfred. *Scholar Mountaineers: Pioneers of Parnassus.* London: Dobson Publishing, 1950.

Peterson, Eugene. *The Message.* NavPress: 2002.

Palmer, Parker J. *On the Brink of Everything: Grace, Gravity, and Getting Old.* Oakland: Berrett-Koehler, 2018.

Perrin, Jim. *Shipton and Tilman: The Great Decade of Himilayan Exploration.* Syracuse, NY: Cornerstone Digital, 2013.

Ridgeway, Rick. *The Big Open: On Foot across Tibet's Chang Tang.* Washington, DC: National Geographic, 2004.

———. *The Shadow of Kilimanjaro: On Foot across East Africa.* New York: Henry Holt, 1998.

Shepherd, Nan. *The Living Mountain: A Celebration of the Cairngorm Mountains of Scotland.* Edinburgh: Canongate Canons, 2011.

www.ingramcontent.com/pod-product-compliance
Lightning Source LLC
Chambersburg PA
CBHW071111090426
42737CB00013B/2566